- MAY 2010

LET'S GET
DRESSED

WRITTEN & ILLUSTRATED BY
RUTH WALTON

W

FRANKLIN WATTS
LONDON•SYDNEY

Every day, when we wake
up in the morning,
we put on our clothes.

What do you put on first?

Can you see it here?

Underneath our other clothes, we wear underwear.

Most underwear is made from **cotton**,
because it's nice and soft.

Do you know what cotton is?

Cotton is a **natural fibre** that comes from cotton plants.
They grow in many countries, including India, China and America.
Cotton is a thirsty plant – it needs lots of water while it's growing!

cotton flower

Cotton creepy-crawlies!

All of these insects love living on cotton plants...

*To kill the insect pests, farmers often use **pesticides** which can harm the environment.*

***Organic** cotton is grown using natural pest controls.*

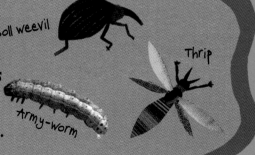

Boll weevil

Thrip

Army-worm

After the plant has flowered, its petals drop off and the seed pods grow. They are called cotton **bolls**.

cotton boll

It takes about 7 to 10 weeks for the cotton bolls to grow fully.

Then the bolls pop open and they are ready to be harvested.

The cotton bolls are soft and fluffy.

7

The cotton is harvested, and taken to a factory to be **processed**.

In the factory, the cotton is washed and spun into **thread**.

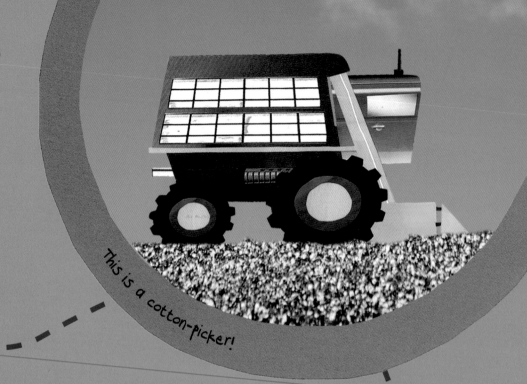

This is a cotton-picker!

The thread can be **woven** on a **loom**, or **knitted** on a machine to become **fabric**.

This fabric is woven...

and this fabric is knitted.

8

The fabric can be **dyed** or printed on with inks to make it colourful.

At a different factory, the fabric is made into clothes, using sewing machines.

It's hard work making clothes!

All of these clothes are made from cotton...

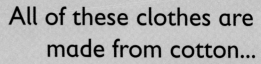

T-shirt

Skirt

Pants

Socks

Jeans

Shirt

Are you wearing any cotton clothes?

9

Most clothes have **fasteners** on them to stop them from falling off! **Zips** and **buttons** are common types of fastener.

Do you know how a zip works?

These are the teeth.

Zips have two small rows of teeth, which lock together when the zipper slides over them, and unlock on the way back.

This is the 'zipper'.

When were zips invented?

Zips were first invented in 1851. Over the next 60 years, several people improved the design of the zip. Finally, in the 1920s and 1930s, zips were at last used on many clothes.

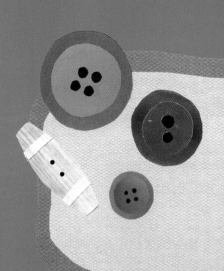

The history of buttons...

Buttons were invented around 3,000 years ago, but were only used as decoration. By the 13th century buttons were being used as fasteners. Before then, people often tied their clothes on with laces — just like we use laces on our shoes!

Are there any fasteners on the clothes you are wearing today?

When it's cold outside, we wear warm clothes.

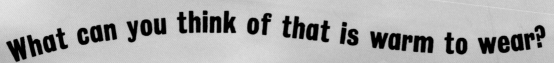

Wool is a natural fibre that is very cosy and good at keeping us snug in cold weather.

Which animal does wool come from?

Goat

Camel

Alpaca

Rabbit

Wool can come from all of these animals!
But most wool we wear comes from **sheep**.

In the winter, sheep grow long coats called **fleeces**, to keep themselves warm.

In the spring, farmers cut the fleeces off the sheep. This is called **shearing**.

The farmer shears the sheep using electric clippers.

He has to hold the sheep tightly so it doesn't escape!

The wool is washed to make sure it's nice and clean.

Here is a farmer shearing his sheep!

Wool can be dyed lots of colours.

When the wool is dry, it is combed to untangle the fibres — just like combing your hair!

Then the wool is spun into **yarn**, and made into clothes.

Most woollen clothes are knitted on a machine.

Knitting can also be done by hand, using knitting needles.

Why do you think knitting takes lots of practice?

You use two needles when you knit by hand.

All of these clothes are made from wool.

Bobble hat

Woolly jacket

Tweed coat

Kilt

Wool can also be woven.

One of the most common fabrics made from woven wool is called **tweed.**

Are you wearing any woollen clothes?

When we go outside, we wear shoes to protect our feet.

Do you know what your shoes are made from?

Most leather comes from cows.

Most shoes are made from **leather**. People make leather by soaking cows' skins in chemicals to make them softer and stronger.

18

The soles of shoes are often made from **rubber,** which is a natural material made from **latex.**

Rubber is very bendy and it is **waterproof**, so it's perfect for keeping your feet dry!

Latex flows from rubber trees - into a bowl!

What else is waterproof to wear?

When it's raining outside, it's good to wear a waterproof coat, or carry an umbrella.

Waterproof fabric is often made from **nylon**.

Do you know what nylon is?

Nylon is a **synthetic** fibre that is made from **oil**.

Oil is a **raw material** that formed under the Earth's surface millions of years ago from dead plants and animals.

This is an oil rig, which is a platform in the sea where the oil is drilled from the sea-bed.

Oil can also come from wells in the ground.

The oil is transported in a ship called an oil tanker.

It is taken to be processed in an **oil refinery.**

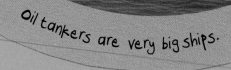

Oil tankers are very big ships.

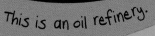

This is an oil refinery.

Some of the oil is mixed with chemicals to make ribbons of nylon.

The ribbons of nylon are melted and pushed through tiny holes, called **spinnerets**, to make thread.

The nylon thread is dried using jets of air, and wound onto reels, ready to be made into fabric.

All of these clothes are made from synthetic fibres...

Acrylic jumper

Polyester shorts

Nylon swimsuit

Nylon anorak

Can you think of any other kinds of fabric?

23

Silkworms like to munch on leaves.

A field of hemp plants.

Silk fabric is soft and thin, but very strong.

Silkworms are the caterpillars of silk moths. They spin the silk fibres.

Silk is very expensive and is a luxury fabric that not many people wear.

Hemp fabric is similar to cotton, but a bit rougher. It comes from plants that are very easy to grow, so it is cheap to make.

It's much better for the environment than cotton as it uses less water and doesn't usually need any pesticides.

Silk is smooth and shiny.

This T-shirt is made from hemp fabric.

Bamboo fibre is thin and stretchy. It is a new kind of fabric made from bamboo, which is a type of grass.

Bamboo grows very quickly. Chemicals are used to turn the plant fibres into fabric.

This bodywarmer is made from polar fleece.

Polar fleece is very soft and good at keeping you warm. It is made from a kind of plastic called polyethylene terephthalate (or PET for short) and it can even be made from recycled water bottles!

Bamboo plants growing.

Can you work out which fabrics are natural, and which are synthetic?

Look them up in the glossary to find out the answers!

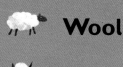 Wool

 Cotton

 Oil

The symbols on the map show the main parts of the world the raw materials for making different fabric come from.

Which is closest to where you live?

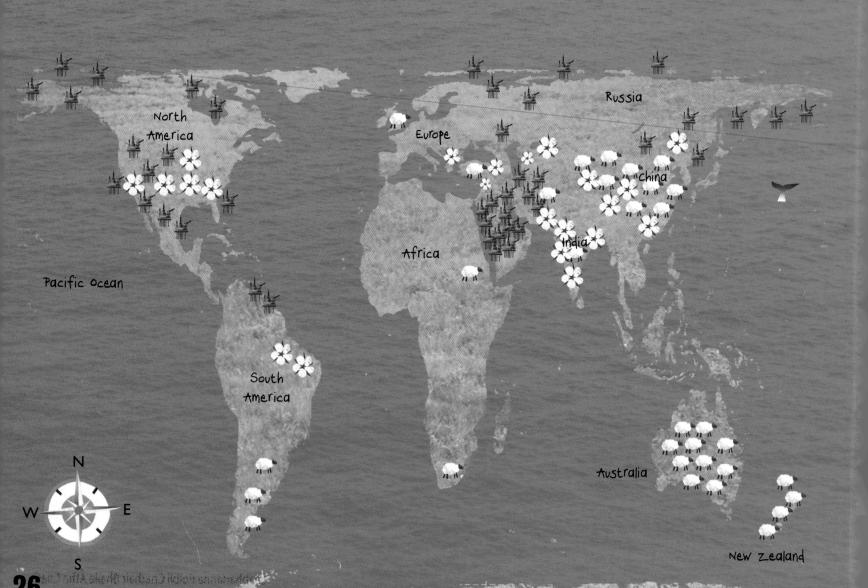

North America

Russia

Europe

China

Africa

India

Pacific Ocean

South America

Australia

New Zealand

Activity:
Have a good look
at what you are
wearing today.

Try to guess what your clothes are made from.
Get a friend to check the label for you — were you right?

Have a look at the map, and see if you can find where it came from.

Glossary

Acrylic a synthetic fibre which feels like wool

Bamboo fibre a type of fabric made from natural fibres of bamboo plants

Boll a fluffy seed pod from the cotton plant

Button a small type of fastener, used by pushing it through a hole

Cotton a natural fibre made from the fluffy seed pods of cotton plants

Dyed when a cloth has been coloured

Fabric cloth, textile or fabric are all woven or knitted materials

Fastener something used for holding fabric together

Fibre a long, thin part of a plant, animal or mineral

Fleece the wool of a sheep before it has been processed

Hemp a fast growing plant used to make natural fibre

Knitted fabric made by looping yarn or thread, using needles or a machine

Latex the sap of rubber trees, used to make rubber

Leather a natural material made from animal skin

Loom a machine used to make woven fabric

Natural existing in nature – not man-made

Nylon a synthetic fibre often used for waterproof clothes

Oil a greasy liquid also called petroleum

Oil refinery a factory where oil is purified

Organic grown without pesticides or other chemicals

Pesticides chemicals used by farmers to kill insects

Polar fleece soft fabric made from synthetic fibres

Polyester a synthetic fibre made from oil

Processed made using a series of different actions

Raw material a material before it has been processed

Rubber a natural material made from latex

Shearing cutting fleeces from sheep to make wool

Sheep grazing animals that grow woolly fleeces

Silk soft cloth made of natural fibres from silkworms

Silkworm caterpillar of the silk moth, which produces silk fibres

Spinneret part of a machine used to make synthetic fibres

Synthetic a man-made material, not found in nature

Thread thin type of string usually made from cotton or nylon

Tweed a type of cloth made from woven wool

Waterproof something that doesn't allow water to get in

Wool a natural fibre made from the fleeces of sheep

Woven fabric made by passing threads over and under each other using a loom

Yarn thread made from wool

Zip a fastener with two rows of teeth that lock together

Index

First published in 2009
by Franklin Watts

Text and illustrations
copyright © Ruth Walton 2009

Franklin Watts
338 Euston Road
London NW1 3BH

Franklin Watts Australia
Level 17/207 Kent Street
Sydney, NSW 2000

Series editor: Sarah Peutrill
Art director: Jonathan Hair
Photographs: Ruth Walton, unless
otherwise credited

Dewey number: 391
ISBN: 978 0 7496 8853 0
Printed in China

Franklin Watts is a division of
Hachette Children's Books, an
Hachette UK company.
www.hachette.co.uk

Picture credits: I Stock Photo:
16b (Madeleine Openshaw), 17t
(Susan Trigg), 18 (Gabriel Eckert),
19b (George Clerk), 22b (Karen
Merryweather), 24tl (Jason
Gulledge), 24tr (ideeone), 25b
(Kevin Russ). Shutterstock: 16t
(Gail Johnson). Every attempt
has been made to clear copyright.
Should there be any inadvertent
omission please apply to the
publisher for rectification.